Middle Gate

Warden's Garden

WINCHESTER

Illustrated by Dennis Page
Written by Rupert Hill

An illustrated stroll through City and College

ACKNOWLEDGEMENTS

Artist's acknowledgements

For permission to wander at will and sketch with abandon I have to thank the Warden, Headmaster and Staff of the College. And for their forbearance and friendly curiosity in what I was up to, I thank the boys.

I owe particular thanks to the Master of Music and his Staff for allowing me to sketch at chamber, jazz and orchestral concerts and recitals. My thanks also to Julian Smith whose Schubert Birthday Evening was a joy to hear and a delight to draw.

I am grateful to Simon Taylor for inviting me to the dress rehearsal of an outstanding production of *King Lear* in the QEII Theatre. To my wife Ann, my special thanks for helping to cool my brushes when they became overheated.

But it is to Sally Milligan and David Fellowes, Director of the Friends, that I owe my greatest thanks. For it was they who first embraced the idea of doing this book and by adroit management and polite nagging were responsible for making it happen.

Dennis Page

Author's Acknowledgements

I am greatly indebted to a considerable number of people who have helped me by providing information, oral or written, historical and otherwise; by arranging access to arcane corners; and by correcting my numerous solecisms, although the errors that remain in this book are entirely my own. I would like to express my warm thanks to: Colin Badcock, Rachel Bebb, Guy Boney, Veronica Cornes, Peter Davis, Katherine Everett, David Fellowes, Roy Grinyer (and all his colleagues in the Porter's Lodge at the College), Graham Hill, Patrick Maclure, Arthur Morgan, Tony Retallack, James Sabben-Clare, Fiona Smith, James Webster and John Wells.

I am particularly grateful to John Thorn for a great deal of his time, advice and corrections, besides also for writing the Foreword; and to John Saumarez-Smith, who found the time in the busy life of a distinguished bookseller to read the text and make a number of most helpful criticisms and suggestions.

My last and largest 'thank you' is to Sally Milligan (who is really the publisher of this book), without whose enthusiasm, encouragement, enterprise and energy this book would never have happened at all – nor without her would its writing have been half as much fun.

Rupert Hill

CONTENTS

FOREWORD

When in 1382 Bishop William of Wykeham founded the College of St Mary, Winchester, he made certain that it was built outside the city walls and that it was independent of the cathedral he was doing so much to beautify. His pupils would go on to his other foundation, New College at Oxford, and would then serve God and England rather than local church and Hampshire. There had never been a school like it.

Winchester College is not short of land. Indeed, some local residents think it has too much. But its presence has ensured that the water meadows on its south side remain a national treasure. It is a school half rural, half urban. The fishing and bird-watching and rowing are on one doorstep, the bustle of a provincial town on the other.

Some townsfolk find it a place of strangers, a self-enclosed academic community whose members scurry around lapping up knowledge and developing skills for several weeks and then go on holidays, leaving the place empty and locked. But this book may help to open some doors, some meadows and fields. Entry has to be controlled, as it must be in all schools. But the school can be visited, and should be. Once inside you will find it not merely beautiful but friendly and hospitable. It is unlike anywhere else in the world.

John Thorn

PREFACE

This book is principally about one part of Winchester, William of Wykeham's College. It is also about the City of Winchester, and its greatest and most famous jewel, the Cathedral. For a relatively small county town, Winchester is uniquely blessed with such a cornucopia of architectural treasures that it would be impossible to guide the visitor to the College alone, and ask him to ignore the other glories of the City. This book, therefore, is a visit to both City and College.

There have been many historical accounts of Winchester – City, Cathedral and College. This present work may contain the odd historical nugget, but it makes no claim to be another history. In the last hundred years or so, Leach, Cook, Firth and Sabben-Clare have been particular adornments of the College's historical canon – notably the most recent history by James Sabben-Clare, published to mark the school's sescentenary in 1982. The keen questing historian can find plenty of other secondary treasures, as well as the College's own remarkable archives, dating right back to the Foundation. For the City in general and the Cathedral in particular, historical works are abundant.

This book will lead the reader from a starting point, the railway station, through the City via the Cathedral to the College, but it does not seek to take the reader round the College itself in an orderly or logical manner. It does not counsel routes or give opening times, although in the best tradition of that doyen of Venetian guidebook writers, the late J G Links, it does not omit helpful directions to essential refreshments and purchases. The dates and measurements which are mentioned are, it is hoped, reliable but not excessive. The information which the book does contain is arbitrarily selected, even idiosyncratically, and is not intended to give a comprehensive picture of the College, either historically or in its modern living form.

Dennis Page is far from the first painter or illustrator to have been charmed by this corner of Winchester. In the nineteenth century Ackermann and then Radclyffe produced their well-known illustrated accounts of the College. The Ackermanns and Radclyffes have mostly been broken up, and their constituent prints of scenes and views of the College have found their way into countless picture frames. So too have Herbert Marshall's pen and ink drawings in 1893, commissioned to commemorate the College's quincentenary. In more recent times, the beauties of the older buildings have been captured by many others.

The illustrations in this book form a contemporary pictorial record of various aspects of the College and the City. The book is a caprice, a companion, a gentle tribute to one of the most beautiful educational environments in England, from a sympathetic and admiring paintbrush, with an accompanying explanation of the various sights and scenes which have captured the artist's eye. It is, if you like, an illustrated stroll.

Outer Gate

1 THE COLLEGE – A BRIEF HISTORY

Statue of the Virgin

William of Wykeham, whose active public life covered the whole of the second half of the fourteenth century, was a very remarkable man. Of humble but able origins, he rose in Edward III's service to be, variously, clerk, surveyor, royal man of affairs, statesman, prelate, twice Lord Chancellor (then the King's principal minister, or today's Prime Minister) under, first, Edward and then Richard II. Most importantly, in terms of his legacy and reputation, he was Bishop of Winchester from 1366 until his death in September 1404.

Today, amid the vicissitudes of a relatively marginalized and impoverished Church, it can be difficult to comprehend the wealth and power of a pre-Reformation Prince of the Church such as the Bishop of Winchester. Wykeham in particular combined the holiness of his Bishopric, the power of a statesman and Prime Minister, and fabulous wealth. It was that wealth which enabled him to found and endow his remarkable double legacy, the sister Colleges of Saint Mary at Oxford and Winchester, better known today as New College, Oxford and Winchester College.

The foundation stone of New College having been laid two years earlier, the construction of the buildings of Winchester College began in 1382, and the College opened its doors to its first Scholars in 1394. Wykeham was an ideal Founder: he had the power and wealth to select and acquire the original five acre site, which lies just outside the old City wall and hard by Wolvesey, the Bishop's palace, and which he bought from the monks of St Swithun's Priory; his experience as a royal surveyor was put to good use in intimate involvement in the design and supervision of the construction of the buildings. As a bishop of the Catholic Church but also very much a 'King's man', he knew exactly what he was seeking to create: not just an institution to enable poor but clever boys to share his own start in life, but also one which, by promoting and expanding the ranks of a well-educated clergy, would reinforce the security of the King's government, for the fourteenth century clergy effectively also provided the civil service and administration of the country.

New College, although magnificent in its appearance and completeness, followed the format and philosophy of earlier Oxford colleges. But in establishing its sister college at Winchester, Wykeham was more revolutionary: the combination of the connection between New College and its own 'feeder' grammar school, and the size, independence and sovereignty of that school was new and unprecedented. Barely fifty years later, King Henry VI's admiration of Wykeham's foundation led him not only to establish Eton College (with its sister college, King's, at Cambridge) but also to take the

Chantry and Cloisters

then Headmaster of Winchester, William Waynflete, to be Eton's first Headmaster, together with several of the Scholars.

The fortunes of Winchester College have fluctuated over the years. It was one thing for Henry VI to take Headmaster and Scholars in order to found Eton. It was quite another matter for the College to survive the widespread dissolution of religious establishments by Henry VIII, and indeed the College probably then came as close to perishing altogether as it has done at any time in its history, being saved only by the King's death in 1547. The Civil War was perilous, and the College was nearly as much at risk as it had been a hundred years earlier. That the College kept its head down and remained completely intact throughout the War, and during the Commonwealth which followed, was largely due to the wisdom of the Warden of the day, Warden Harris. As Firth's history has it, the net cost of the War to the College was "£28 16s 0d for compulsory billeting and a few years deprivation of organicall music".

Shortly after the Restoration, the College was completely evacuated from Winchester to neighbouring Crawley on account of the plague of 1666. There were two great school rebellions in 1793 and 1818, both during the long tenure of Warden Huntingford, the first coinciding with revolution in France and the second with widespread social unrest in England. Indeed, the Gallic Red Cap of Liberty flew briefly over Outer Gate during the 1793 rebellion, which was probably the inevitable culmination of the indiscipline and harshness prevailing under the late eighteenth century Wykehamical regime. Substantial reforms followed the intervention of the University Commissioners in the 1850's and the Clarendon Commission on the Public Schools in 1862. In the 1960's, there were well-founded fears that the then Labour Government would seek to abolish the public schools altogether, and more insidious attacks continue to be made by the present Government, notably by way of threats to the public schools' charitable status.

Despite all that turbulence, however, the same school has survived for over six centuries, without any interruption, in the same premises, and for the benefit of the same body of seventy Scholars. It is the oldest school in England with an unbroken existence since its foundation. That alone is a very remarkable achievement, which might by itself justify our visit, but perhaps even more important in the context of our stroll is the fact that most of Wykeham's fourteenth century buildings have survived and are still being used, many for exactly the purposes which he intended. The buildings and their location, still on the edge of the town, hard by the Cathedral and with the River Itchen and St Catherine's Hill running away to the south-east, make for one of the loveliest of school settings. And not only the buildings have survived: the Warden, ten Fellows, two masters, seventy Scholars, three chaplains and sixteen

Quiristers contemplated by Wykeham's Statutes are all still present today, even if their numbers have been augmented by over six hundred boys and many more teaching and administrative staff.

It is not only the fortunes but also the academic reputation of the school which have varied over the centuries. The College could be said in very broad terms to have flourished in its first 150 years, but declined into relative academic obscurity during much of the three centuries from the reign of the first Elizabeth until the reforming Commissions of the 1850's and 1860's, before being revived again by a combination of the competitive exams introduced by those reforms and a succession of successful Victorian headmasters, pre-eminent among them being Dr Ridding, now honoured by the accolade "the Second Founder". The modern Wykehamist, as Wykeham's pupils are known, and in particular today's Winchester Scholar, admitted to the College only after daunting examination, would hardly recognize his pre-1850 predecessor: his forebear's place would most likely have been secured by patronage, and the exam would have been little more than farce, with a couple of lines of Ovid for translation from the Latin, and to the traditional question "can you sing?" the invariable traditional reply "yes Sir: all people that on earth do dwell".

Nowadays the College flourishes as a centre of academic excellence which, in the realms of secondary education, is generally acknowledged to be without peer in England. It has a reputation for producing 'clever' Wykehamists, although that is by no means an exclusively complimentary term of admiration. It does not seek to churn out examinational successes or to top exam league tables; rather, it *does* tend to top exam league tables (except when they are "fixed" by Government), but only incidentally to the College's real purpose, which is to educate in the round, and to broaden the mind. It does not produce Prime Ministers (only one – excluding pre-Reformation Chancellors like Wykeham himself – to Eton's current tally of nineteen, and that one was Henry Addington of whom the doggerel cruelly ran "Pitt is to Addington as London is to Paddington"), and the typical successful Wykehamist is traditionally thought to be more likely to be a judge or a Permanent Secretary than a 'captain of industry' or a conspicuous star in the public constellation. But scratch only lightly on the surface of first assumptions, and Wykehamists living and dead pop up in countless different walks of life: Richard Noble, the *quondam* world land speed record holder, and the Nawab of Pataudi, the former Indian cricket captain, were the most recent Wykehamist honorands at the "*Ad Portas*" ceremony which will be mentioned later. Like them, most Wykehamists are usually rather successful, and united by being the beneficiaries of the excellence of Wykeham's education and of the constant practical application of his precept and motto for the College, "*Manners Makyth Man*".

New College, Oxford

Westgate

2 FROM THE STATION TO THE CATHEDRAL

The days of steam on Southern Region are long gone, alas, but there is at least the compensation that a shiny new 'Wessex Flyer' of South West Trains takes less than an hour from Waterloo to Winchester Station. The Station is only ten minutes' walk from the centre of town, and barely twenty minutes on foot from the College itself.

A lot happens in Winchester nowadays, apart from the College. Modern Winchester is a prosperous, thriving county town, with a population of about 36,000. It is the home of Hampshire County Council as well as the seat of the City Council. It houses the principal Law Courts on the Western Circuit, and a number of supporting legal practices. It has a major prison, the County police headquarters and the Royal Hampshire County Hospital. There is a great deal of education: Peter Symonds, Winchester's (other) Sixth Form College; St Swithun's, the distinguished girls' school; the Winchester College of Art; and the University of Winchester (better known in the past as King Alfred's Teacher Training College, and latterly as University College of Winchester), with ten times as many students as Winchester College.

But in addition to all its modern assets and functions, Winchester has its history and – for a not very large county town – glorious and varied architectural treasures. As its buildings and ruins so vividly show, Winchester has been a civilized settlement for the best part of two millennia. Pevsner understandably describes Winchester, with its combination of Cathedral, College, Great Hall, and Wolvesey Palace, and with St Cross a mile to the south, as the richest architecturally of all English bishops' sees. Winchester's history is as distinguished and rich as that of any other city in England outside London. Many of those treasures can be seen on the walk down the hill to the College.

A short distance from the Station, we leave the railway line, and at the bottom of Upper High Street meet the 1759 obelisk commemorating "the widows and orphans who died in the Great Plague" of 1666 (the year after the more famous London plague). Just below the obelisk stands the thirteenth century Westgate, the western entrance to the old mediaeval city: a short climb to its parapet permits a survey of the rooftops of central Winchester, and the complete length of the High Street.

Immediately to the north of the Westgate are the 1960 County Council offices. Neo-Georgian and red brick, they have complemented in a remarkably inoffensive and timeless way the older Winchester townscape. One only has to think of the dismal Holford 1960's development of Paternoster Square in the very shadow of Sir Christopher Wren's masterpiece, St Paul's Cathedral, or the even more dreadful (and thankfully now also demolished) Department of the Environment buildings in

Buttercross

15

Marsham Street, Westminster, to appreciate Winchester's relatively good fortune in its civic architecture.

On the grass outside the main entrance of County Hall, there grazes an imposing pig, or rather an elegant bronze cast of the 'Hampshire Hog', by David Kemp, commemorating the centenary of Hampshire County Council in 1989. To the south of the Westgate is Henry III's Great Hall, built between 1222 and 1236, a double cube of 110 by 55 by 55 feet, and housing on its west wall King Arthur's Round Table, with its Tudor rose in its middle and the knights' names inscribed in black round the circumference. Before heady visions of Camelot arise, the Table too was made not earlier than the thirteenth century, or about 700 years after King Arthur's legendary time, and quite possibly only much later still. Until the new Law Courts were built in the early 1970's immediately to the east of the Great Hall, the Hall was the seat of Winchester's Assize Court.

Still at the top of the town, and beyond the Great Hall, is the site of the former Barracks. We shall meet Wren (or his influence) again later in this stroll, but his principal commission in Winchester was his engagement by Charles II, near the end of the Carolean reign, to build the King's House. This would have been a vast and grandiose palace, an English mini-Versailles, but work stopped on the death of its royal patron in 1685, and the original project was never completed. Such of the work as had been completed was later converted and extended into barracks, which were destroyed by fire in 1894. The most recent barrack buildings date from around 1900, and have themselves evolved in the 1990's into an elegant residential *quartier* following the departure of the Army after over two centuries' residence in Winchester. Tangible

Hampshire Hog

Great Hall and King Arthur's Round Table

King Alfred

shades of the Army still remain: there are the Regimental Headquarters of the Royal Green Jackets and several Regimental Museums, but the Regular battalions of the RGJ have departed elsewhere.

Passing through the Westgate, long closed to vehicles, the High Street stretches downhill, as it has done since mediaeval times. Almost immediately on the right is another bronze statue – this time, a typically powerful representation of a mounted horseman by Elizabeth Frink in 1975. Further down, conspicuously jutting over the High Street just below the point where it becomes pedestrianized, is a large clock, attached to the former Guildhall of 1713, with its elegant Queen Anne façade and indeed a statue of Queen Anne over the door (possibly the only branch of Lloyds Bank to be so endowed). Opposite is the God Begot House, a heavily restored timber-framed building, but still with sixteenth century traces.

We could continue down the High Street, to admire the Victorian splendour of the present Guildhall, built in 1871, or even proceed right to the bottom and pay our respects to King Alfred, a large and imposing bronze by Hamo Thornycroft which the more eagle-eyed may just have espied from the parapet of the Westgate. Erected in 1901, the statue was intended to mark the millennial anniversary of Alfred's death, but it is now generally agreed that Alfred died in 899 and that the gesture was two years late. It would be possible to succumb to any number of retail opportunities. But at the Buttercross, erected in the fifteenth century and largely restored by Sir Giles Gilbert Scott in 1865, we shall turn right through a covered passageway to The Square, passing the completely enclosed church of St Lawrence on the left and the vestigial remains of the old Norman Palace.

Notwithstanding the attractions of the City Museum, on the corner of The Square, including the site of Winchester's last public execution, the beheading of Dame Alice Lisle on 2 September 1685 as part of Judge Jeffreys' infamous retribution for the failed Monmouth Rebellion, we shall continue under the lime trees down the stone-flagged path to the west end of the Cathedral. Away to the right of the path is the memorial to the unfortunate end of Thomas Thetcher, a Grenadier in the North Hants Militia, "who died of a violent Fever contracted by drinking Small Beer when hot" in 1764. The stone has been replaced three times by subsequent Regiments, with the charming reminder that "An honest Soldier never is forgot Whether he die by Musket or by Pot". Among the cluster of twentieth century military memorials outside the West Door of the Cathedral are the Rifleman commemorating the dead of the King's Royal Rifle Corps (the 60th) during the two World Wars, and the tribute to the 737 lost on *HMS Hampshire* when she was sunk by a mine off the Orkney Islands on 5 June 1916 – among them Lord Kitchener.

Frink Horse in the High Street

3 CATHEDRAL AND CLOSE

Winchester was the capital of Wessex, from the reign of King Egbert in the early ninth century until the Norman Conquest, by which time it was effectively also the capital of England. Saxon Winchester was also a major bishopric, and an important religious centre. There were, remarkably, two contemporaneous Minsters substantially on the site of the present Cathedral: the earlier of them (not surprisingly, the Old Minster) dated from the seventh century, and its footprint can still be seen marked by the stones in the grass on the north side of the Nave.

It was the Normans who built the present Cathedral, just under a thousand years ago. Rebuilt in part (the first tower fell down soon after it was erected, in 1107), altered on several occasions over the next 400 years (notably by William of Wykeham, who remodelled most of the Cathedral in the Perpendicular style, apart from the Transepts) and restored in the nineteenth and twentieth centuries, latterly by the complete underpinning of the east end foundations (the original foundations having been set on a timber raft on a bog), the Cathedral's external length of 556 feet makes it the longest cathedral in England and Europe, even if its nave is pipped for length by St Peter's in Rome.

Unlike Salisbury with its graceful spire, or Durham with its commanding hill, or Ely "the ship of the Fens", to mention but three others, Winchester Cathedral hides its external light under something of a reluctant bushel, and its huge size is not readily visible from outside (although St Catherine's Hill, later in this stroll, will provide an exceptional viewing point): it is only from the inside that the immense length and majesty of the Cathedral become so forcefully apparent, and that we can appreciate that this is one of the most beautiful buildings in England.

We shall enter by the West Door (or rather by the smaller side door leading into the North Aisle). Our purpose today does not include a detailed tour of the Cathedral, and we shall not stay long. But even a stroll the full length of the North Aisle to the Lady Chapel at the east end and a return by the South Aisle to the South Door, with the odd diversion, will amply repay the visit.

If we move immediately into the Nave and are very lucky, all the seating will have been removed, and the Nave will be seen at its very starkest and best, in all its Gothic splendour. Back in the North Aisle, there is the tomb of Jane Austen, and its accompanying original modest memorial tribute (interments within the Cathedral itself ceased after 1850). The Norman simplicity of the North Transept is largely untouched, save for the painted ceilings, which are early nineteenth century. From the North Transept we may descend to the Crypt: even if a full tour is impossible because the

Cathedral Nave

Crypt is flooded, there is at least the consolation of seeing Anthony Gormley's statue "Sound II" (modelled on himself) almost seeming to stand on the surface of the water.

Out of the Crypt, and continuing along the North Presbytery Aisle, we pass Bishop Gardner's Chantry. Gardner's episcopate was during those turbulent Tudor times: he was appointed by Henry VIII, removed and imprisoned by Edward VI, and reappointed by Mary, whom he also served as Lord Chancellor. He also officiated at Mary's marriage to Philip of Spain in this Cathedral on 25 July 1554: one of the greater 'what if's ...?' of English history is the childlessness of that uncompromisingly Catholic union. Beyond Gardner's Chantry, the thirteenth century floor tiles are the largest and oldest area of indoor tiling to survive in England. There are also the Chantries of William of Wykeham's two immediate successors as Bishop, Cardinal Beaufort and William Waynflete. Between them, those three occupied the See of Winchester for nearly 120 years: in those pre-Reformation days, the Bishops of Winchester were hugely powerful and wealthy men, and each of those episcopal potentates was also Chancellor of England – Wykeham twice and Beaufort three times.

Between the two episcopal Chantries is the Monument to St Swithun, whom we shall meet again shortly. To the right of the Lady Chapel at the extreme east end is the bronze bust of the "Winchester Diver", William Walker, whose underwater exertions

William of Wykeham

Anthony Gormley's 'Sound II'

between 1906–1911 signally contributed to the securing of the Cathedral's foundations and the rescue of the building from complete collapse. Returning along the South Presbytery Aisle, we see the mortuary boxes on top of the screens on both sides, containing the alleged remains of Saxon Kings, including Cnut (or Canute, if you prefer) of tidal fame. The last King of England to be buried in the Cathedral was William Rufus, whose original burial under the tower in 1100 was said to have caused its collapse. Where William's remains are now, no one knows.

On to the Choir, where the wooden choir stalls date from the fourteenth century. Fortunately the delightful misericords – the carved wooden supports under the tip-up

Deanery

Misericords

seats – survived the Puritan iconoclasm of the Civil War. In early times, all participants were required to stand throughout services. With nine services a day in the original Benedictine foundation at Winchester, this was an onerous business for elderly and infirm monks, and by the early twelfth century it had become customary to provide these tip-up seats with their additional support for the standing monks; from the act of mercy – *misericordia* – came the name. In the 68 stalls, 66 mediaeval misericords survive, and the missing two were replaced in 1990 – from Australia. Each misericord has its own carved embellishment – ornate, often amusing, sometimes even lewd, all delightful.

From the Choir, looking back along the nave, there can be seen the kaleidoscope of glass in the great West Window, all replaced like a vitreous patchwork quilt after the destruction of the original window by Cromwell's troops in the Civil War. As we step down from the altar to return to the South Transept, we pass the Ship's Bell of the previous HMS *Iron Duke*, Admiral Jellicoe's flagship at Jutland. In the South Transept itself, we may pause at the delightful memorial to Isaak Walton, who is buried in, appropriately, the Fishermen-Apostles' Chapel, before we climb the stairs to visit the Library and the Triforium Gallery. In the former are Bishop Morley's remarkable library from the seventeenth century and some of the Cathedral's art treasures, including in particular its most precious possession, the twelfth century illuminated Winchester Bible. From the latter, at the second level of the three storey Norman elevation of the Transept, there is a wonderful view of the interior of the Cathedral, and a display of various statues and other artefacts. Of particular note are the chair in which Mary allegedly sat during her marriage to Philip of Spain, and the plaque recording the Cathedral's gratitude to its principal benefactors whose support has permitted the restoration of the Gallery and Library: at the top of a distinguished list is Mr Al Gordon – New Yorker, centenarian, Honorary Fellow of the College and munificent philanthropist, whose generosity to the College and the Cathedral has been unparalleled.

As we return towards the South Door, the profusion of military memorials along both Aisles provides a constant reminder of Winchester's martial past. And before leaving of course, we must also pay our respects to William of Wykeham, at his Chantry just to the west of the South Door.

The South Door leads directly into the Close. We pass the Deanery on our left: this is the successor to the mediaeval Prior's House, whose thirteenth century porch still survives, as too does the fifteenth century Prior's Hall, even if subsequently greatly altered. The (visiting High Court) Judges' Lodgings are to the right: although the majesty isolation of the senior judiciary is being steadily eroded, and itinerant judges are ever more likely to be billeted in hotels, Winchester is one of the few provincial law centres still to keep its Judges' Lodgings. We pass by the Pilgrims School, a prep school

Cathedral Choir

which not only sends many of its alumni on to the College but also contributes to the education of the sixteen Quiristers, or young choristers, who sing in the College Chapel; it is also the Choir School for the Cathedral. Some may admire the 1966 metal sculpture by Barbara Hepworth on the grass outside the Deanery: "Construction (Crucifixion) – homage to [Piet] Mondrian". In the south-east corner of the Close, the

The Priory Stabling

early fourteenth century Pilgrims' Hall, as it is now known, has the earliest surviving hammer-beam roof. Cheyney Court, the pretty Elizabethan timber-framed building just inside the southern gateway to the Close, served as the Bishop's Courthouse, and now incorporates the Porter's Lodge.

Leaving the Close by that southern gateway, we are in St Swithun Street, hard by Kingsgate, and at the beginning of our visit to the College itself.

Cheyney Court

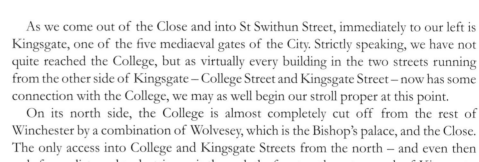

4 GATEWAYS AND ENTRANCES

As we come out of the Close and into St Swithun Street, immediately to our left is Kingsgate, one of the five mediaeval gates of the City. Strictly speaking, we have not quite reached the College, but as virtually every building in the two streets running from the other side of Kingsgate – College Street and Kingsgate Street – now has some connection with the College, we may as well begin our stroll proper at this point.

On its north side, the College is almost completely cut off from the rest of Winchester by a combination of Wolvesey, which is the Bishop's palace, and the Close. The only access into College and Kingsgate Streets from the north – and even then only for cyclists and pedestrians – is through the fourteenth century arch of Kingsgate. By the pedestrian passageway on its east side is a print shop. Above the gateway is the tiny church of St Swithun, who was a ninth century Saxon Bishop of Winchester and very much a Hampshire saint. He was also a great builder, including among his works a bridge across the Itchen at the east end of the town which, the Dictionary of National Biography (OUP, 1975) records, excited much admiration. His famed kindness is illustrated by the legend of his making whole a basketful of eggs carried by a market-woman that was broken on his bridge. The ancient belief in the influence of St Swithun's Day (15 July) upon the succeeding weather is expressed in the verse:

> St Swithun's day, if thou dost rain
> For forty days it will remain;
> St Swithun's day, if thou be fair,
> For forty days 't will rain na mair.

And of course he is also commemorated by the girls' school bearing his name, on the outskirts of Winchester, but that falls outside the scope of this book.

Passing under Kingsgate, we turn left into College Street. A photograph of the procession from College to Cathedral for the quincentennial celebration service in 1893 shows houses and shops along both sides of the street; a century later, the only surviving building on the north side of the street is the College Bursary. On the south side, we come to Outer Gate, the original main entrance to the mediaeval foundation and still today the Porters' Lodge, the nerve centre of the College security system, and the starting point of more expert guided tours of the College. The statue of the Virgin in the niche above the gateway reminds the visitor that this is, strictly, the College of St Mary at Winton. Inside the gateway on the east wall, a single notice records the names

Kingsgate and St. Swithun's

of the fifteen or so young gentlemen 'elected' in the current year's 'Election Exam' to scholarships – that is, to places in College itself, the original mediaeval institution, subsidized by the Foundation, as opposed to the ten nineteenth century 'Commoner' houses, which account for ninety percent of the boys in the school. A solid and imposing gateway, and when its gates are shut, a secure one too: from the long blank wall of the old Brewery running back along College Street from Outer Gate, security must have been as important to Wykeham himself as, sadly, it has again become to his twenty-first century successors.

We will enter the College in a moment, but let us first pass by Outer Gate and continue along College Street. It will give us a chance at least to glimpse another work of Wren: Wolvesey, the Bishop's palace, built in 1684, the year after Wren was engaged to build the King's House, whose shades we passed on our way down from the Station. Following the College's wall, we turn right into College Walk, and then right again alongside a rather austere and unadorned building, imaginatively named New Hall. If it suggests a 1950's-1960's provenance, it will have spoken honestly (the County Council offices are its exact contemporary), but otherwise we shall ignore it, for it will be visited later. We cross Logie, a pleasant culverted stream, now running as clear as any European Directive could desire, but formerly the open sewer for the buildings on the east side of the College. Ahead of us is Non Licet Gate, leading into Meads, the innermost and oldest of the College's playing fields. By the end of the nineteenth century, Non Licet Gate was kept permanently shut, except during the summer term when bathing (in Old Barge, as the Itchen was known to the school, in a spot nearby called Gunner's Hole) was 'licet' or permitted. One of the College's many unsubstantiated traditions has it that, when a boy was expelled, he was ejected through Non Licet Gate and his clothes and possessions were thrown over the wall after him; sadly actuality is more prosaic, and there is no recorded instance of such a dramatic end to a Wykehamist education.

Alternatively, from Kingsgate the visitor may proceed straight ahead down Kingsgate Street, which Pevsner understandably describes as very rewarding. Resisting the early temptation of refreshment in The Wykeham Arms (but we will return there later), we pass a number of very agreeable-looking Georgian houses, now mostly occupied by the teaching staff. Number 5 dates from c 1700; number 70 has a delightful double-bow shopfront, and used to house the school tailors until the 1960's; number 69 is Moberly's, the oldest of the Commoner houses, with origins dated 1571.

Opposite number 62 (now the Headmaster's house) we find an imposing gateway on the left (east) side of the street. This is Commoner Gate, with the College's South Africa War Memorial, built immediately after that war, and having a foundation stone

Wolvesey and the Cathedral

30

laid in October 1902 by Field Marshal Lord Roberts, who had commanded the Army in South Africa and was then the British Army's last Commander-in-Chief, the post being abolished on his retirement. Perhaps rather remarkably for such a supposedly cerebral school, Winchester has produced five Field Marshals (a tally beaten only by Eton and Westminster), even though 'Bobs' was not among that select number.

On further down Kingsgate Street, past Arts and Sciences, and on the left, an open vista of unbuilt greenery: through Altham Gates (erected in 1971 in memory of Harry Altham, Housemaster, President of the MCC, and distinguished doyen of twentieth century Wykehamist cricket), a view over the 1st XI cricket field, the Itchen and the water-meadows, to St Catherine's Hill beyond.

Chapel

5 CHAMBER COURT AND CHAPEL

Let us choose Outer Gate, and pass through it into Outer Court. We will come back both to the much later Warden's Lodgings (not so much 'lodgings' as an extremely elegant and large residence, behind its rather forbidding exterior) on the left, and to Moberly Library, behind us to the right in the old Brewery. Pass through Middle Gate – Inner Gate seems never to have entered the Wykehamical lexicon – and we are at once at the heart of the original mediaeval foundation, in Chamber Court.

It is not known to what extent Wykeham was his own architect, but he would have been more than competent to be intimately involved in the detailed design of the original College buildings. Wykeham could be said to have made his name, and secured his subsequent ascendancy, by his success as Supervisor of the Works at Windsor Castle when it was rebuilt by Edward III. Here at Winchester one can but admire the compactness and simplicity, the logic and effectiveness, of the one and a half acres of buildings, centred on this small (less than forty yards square) but very beautiful quadrangle, which is easily the peer of many of its counterparts at Oxford and Cambridge.

Chamber Court and the buildings round it have looked much the same for over six hundred years. The square Chapel tower was erected in the fifteenth century, to replace the original round tower with its spire. The top storey mansard windows in the previously two-storey buildings on the west, north and east sides of the quadrangle date from the nineteenth century. The north-facing exterior of the Chapel itself has just been cleaned, in 2004: thanks to the lime and stonedust 'shelter coat' which was applied during the cleaning process in order to stabilize and strengthen the softer stone underneath, the exterior is now a rather brilliant white, with an almost ghostly appearance in the dark (substantial work, at even more substantial expense, remains to be done to the south and east faces, and to the south face of Hall). The ante-chapel's aluminium and glass doors were installed in 1967, and the passageway immediately to their right was only created three hundred years after the Foundation. But otherwise the visitor sees pretty much what the first Scholars would have seen in 1394.

Not only does the visitor see much the same buildings, but they are still used for substantially the same purposes as they have been for the last six hundred years. Admittedly the Warden, ten Fellows, three Chaplains and sixteen Quiristers no longer have to be accommodated in the 'Chambers' around the quadrangle, as they did in the beginning, and the seventy Scholars have to share the premises only with the Master in College and his family. But the Scholars still study in the six ground floor Chambers, and sleep upstairs. This is no museum: these buildings have always worked for their living.

On the south side of Chamber Court are the two principal buildings, Hall and Chapel (Wykehamists, like Yorkshiremen, have a strange predilection for dropping the definite article). Unlike the buildings on the other three sides, which are of flint with stone mullions and a slate roof, Hall and Chapel are constructed entirely of ashlar, and mostly from stone brought by sea from the Bere quarry in Devon. For these buildings, only the best would do. Nevertheless, despite its lovely proportions, Hall lacks the atmosphere of its Oxford and Cambridge equivalents: too much boiled cabbage and not enough 'High Table', except on rare occasions like Old Wykehamist dinners. But if the Warden and Fellows have no longer dined there as a matter of course since they ceased to reside in College after the Reformation, others of Wykeham's strictures in his original Statutes are still observed: grace is still said in Latin every day by the Prefect of Hall, '*Aulae Praefectus*', as the head Scholar (and *ipso facto* head of the school) is still known.

Appropriately, perhaps, for the very heart of the original Foundation, Chamber Court is the only place within the College campus which hosts assemblies of the entire school as a single body (although we will later find the site of another, *alfresco* assembly on St Catherine's Hill). Once every four or five years, or a little more often if necessary to accommodate Royalty or great anniversaries, the College honours a distinguished

Chamber Court and Chapel

Hall

Chapel Tower

visitor – usually an eminent Old Wykehamist – by receiving him '*Ad Portas',* or loosely 'at the Gates'. The visitor enters by Middle Gate, flanked by the Warden, Headmaster, Fellows and staff; the school lines the other three sides of Chamber Court, with the Scholars in the middle along Chapel wall. The Prefect of Hall addresses the honorand in Latin, to which the honorand used normally to reply in the same tongue, even if his speech too had been written by the Prefect of Hall. More recently the language of Cromwell, as Field Marshal Lord Carver put it at his '*Ad Portas',* has tended to displace the language of Caesar, although Latin was made unusually modern to the English schoolboy ear by Lord Clark's fluent Italian pronunciation at his own reception. Upon the remarkable occasion in 1981 when the honorands were ten Wykehamist senior judges, the combination of judicial robes and the gowns and hoods of the Fellows and dons in full academic fig made for a memorable and colourful spectacle.

The dominant adjacent building is Chapel. The College is a mediaeval ecclesiastical foundation: Chapel was absolutely central and fundamental to the school as a whole. While its relative importance may have diminished by the seventh century of the College's existence – perhaps inevitably in this much more secular age, with the vast number of academic subjects and other activities now offered by the College – Chapel still remains the most imposing building on the school campus.

There is, then, a certain paradox to its also being the building which, of all the original mediaeval Foundation, would be least recognized by Wykeham, were he to return today and step inside. True, it still has the same elegant proportions, and the same fine wooden cusped lierne-vaulted ceiling. But otherwise there is no great architectural purity to the interior, which has seen three main and quite distinct internal orders. The present pews, the gloomy panelling along the north and south sides, and the west gallery and organ loft are all early twentieth century, and are the sequel by W D Caröe to the remodelling of the interior begun by William Butterfield in the 1870's, not least in order to accommodate the much larger numbers of boys resulting from the establishment of the modern 'Commoner' houses. That remodelling was consequent upon the aesthetically disastrous decision to strip out the 1680's panelling by Edward Pierce, although that story had a happy ending of sorts which we will meet later in New Hall. Before the 1680's panelling was commissioned by Warden Nicholas, the visitor would have found the original unpanelled stone interior, including the 15th century reredos, which was restored, or recreated, by Butterfield (but with Caröe's subsequent alterations in the centre, notably the Great War soldier). The 1870's reorganization might well have seen the hand of Sir Giles Gilbert Scott, but he declined the commission since Butterfield was by then well installed as architect-in-residence at the College.

The other notable feature inside Chapel is the glass in the east window. The original famous Jesse Window, dating back to the Foundation, was taken out for cleaning in the early 1820's: by the time Ackermann saw it in 1816 (when, fortunately for posterity, he recorded the Pierce panelling *in situ*, as did Radclyffe 30 years later), it was evidently pretty indecipherably grubby. The mediaeval glass was then dispersed and lost, and the present, rather more clearly defined window dates from 1823. But not lost completely: a combination of painstaking detective work, the aesthetic drive of the then Headmaster Dr Oakeshott, and the generosity of, in particular, Lord (Kenneth) Clark (of 'Civilisation' fame, himself a Wykehamist, and father of the flamboyant diarist and lothario, Alan, himself an Etonian), resulted in the recovery of several panels of the original glass and their installation in 1951 in honour of Dr Rendall, the Headmaster from 1911 to 1924, in (Warden) Thurburn's Chantry on the south side of the Chapel nave. Other panels from the original window have been installed in Fromond's Chantry, which we shall be visiting shortly.

Before we leave Chamber Court by Seventh Chamber Passage, a very brief detour yields perhaps the most peculiar and well-known of Wykehamical treasures, "that bizarre but universally popular figure", the Trusty Servant. Immediately to the right of the staircase up to College Hall, a passageway leads to the old Beer Store (now the Treasury). In front of us, as we enter the passageway, is the Trusty Servant's portrait. First appearing in sixteenth century costume in the manuscript of '*De Collegiata Schola [Wiccamica]*', he has been repainted several times, and in 1778 was given his present Windsor blue livery in honour of a visit by King George III. The present portrait was painted in 1809. The attribution of the accompanying verses which both honour and explain the Trusty Servant are typically uncertain, but Christopher Johnson, a late sixteenth century Headmaster, probably lays best claim to the original Latin. But for those of us who can only cope with the vernacular and not the Vulgate …

Trusty Se...

> *A Trusty Servant's portrait would you see,*
> *This Emblematic Figure well survey.*
> *The Porker's Snout, not nice in diet shews;*
> *The Padlock shut, no secret he'll disclose;*
> *Patient, the Ass, his master's wrath will bear;*
> *Swiftness in errand, his Staggs Feet declare;*
> *Loaded his left hand, apt to labour saith;*
> *The Vest, his neatness; Open Hand, his faith;*
> *Girt with his Sword, his Shield upon his arm,*
> *Himself and master he'll protect from harm*

Staircase to College Hall

6 CLOISTERS AND CHANTRY

Immediately to the south of Chapel are Cloisters, built as part of the original Foundation to be the burial ground of the College, and consecrated on the same day as Chapel, on 17 July 1395.

Cloisters are not in architectural axis with the main body of mediaeval buildings around Chamber Court, and despite their physical proximity to those buildings they have a remarkable feeling of seclusion, even of separation, from the rest of the College. There are no openings in the outer walls apart from the entrance gates in the north-west corner, a small doorway in the north side leading to Chapel tower, and a third small wicket gate in the east wall, called Bell Gate after a housemaster killed in the Great War. Bell Gate is almost always locked, but through its grille there is a tantalizing view of the Warden's Garden, another scene of comparable tranquillity which we shall visit later.

Cloisters are secluded; indeed they are hardly frequented at all, and the visitor has every chance of making a solitary perambulation. Cloisters are cool, and they have given their name to the school's summer term – Cloister Time – because in the heat of the summer the Scholars were permitted to take their lessons in Cloisters instead of in the oppressive heat of the packed schoolroom. With their high wagon roofs, whose original fourteenth century beams create the impression of long inverted wooden ships' hulls, Cloisters have more of a foreign feel to them than any other part of the College.

Around the walls are memorial plaques: half a length of wall bearing the names of some remarkably distinguished Wykehamists who, on closer inspection, all turn out to have been Wardens, or chairmen of the school governors in modern parlance; another section of wall devoted, a little oddly, to successive Bursars. A plaque on the north wall commemorates Winchester's most distinguished soldier, Wavell, third of the five Field Marshals, and a single stone with his name, set in the grass within the Cloisters, marks his grave. Wavell was a Scholar, and a clever one, in an age (the last five years of the nineteenth century) when clever Scholars were not expected to become soldiers; indeed, Winchester has never been a 'military' school, notwithstanding numerous Wykehamist soldiers. Upon the young Wavell declaring his wish to join the Army Class, Dr Fearon the Headmaster wrote to Colonel Wavell, pointing out that there was no need to take the drastic step of putting his son in the Army, "since I believe he has sufficient brains to make his way in other walks of life". As Wavell observed long afterwards, "not a very tactful letter, perhaps, to a soldier, the son of a soldier . . .".

Cloisters

Cloisters' Gates

Bell Gate

Other individual plaques remind the visitor of frailties and perils, and the brevity of lives: a memorial to a "... Commoner of this College from September 1916 who lost his life on October 10 1918 [aged 15] in the Irish Channel when returning to school on the steamship *Leinster* which was sunk by a German submarine"; or to another Commoner who "... died 23 September 1942 aged 16 from an injury in canvas [the College's own form of football]. On him be the peace and the blessing for he was greathearted"; or most poignant for brevity, in memory of a Scholar "... born June 3 1899. For three weeks scholar of this College. God called him on St Luke's Day 1912".

Two memorials particularly catch the eye, one for its ethereal quality, the other for its display of early Wykehamist self-confidence in the Wykehamist's place in life. The former is the memorial "To the glory of God and in proud memory of George Herbert Leigh Mallory Scholar of this College MCM – V Who was lost to human sight between Heaven and Earth While attempting to reach the summit of Mount Everest On June VIII MCMXXIV". The other is the actual tombstone in the south-east corner, recording that "*Hoc sub marmore sepultus est / Tho Welsted / Quem calculi ictu mors / Prostravit. In hac schola / Primus erat Nec / Ut speramus in caelo ultimus est / Quod pro Oxonio adiit / 13 Die Januarii / Anno Domini 1676 [anno] Aetatis sua 18*" *.

In the middle of Cloisters, built as an early fifteenth century addition, is Chantry. It was erected and endowed by John Fromond, Steward of the Manors, for the celebration of masses for the repose of his soul. It was consecrated in 1437, and formally accepted by the College on 20 June 1446. Chantry is a very rare example of a chapel standing inside a cloister. In the Perpendicular style, it is like Chapel built of ashlar, although the authorities appear to be divided on the Bere or Ventnor provenance of the stone. In the east window are seven more figures from the Founder's original Jesse Window in Chapel, five as an American gift in memory of the US Army forces quartered in Winchester in 1917–18, and the other two repatriated from the parish church of Coleorton, near Ashby-de-la-Zouch in Leicestershire.

Like other more recent buildings in the College which we shall visit, Chantry's uses have changed through the ages. Fromond's masses (celebrated annually on the anniversary of his death on 20 November 1420) passed away with the Reformation, by virtue of the Statutes of 1546 and 1547 for the general suppression of chantries, although they enjoyed a brief revival under our last overtly Catholic monarch, Mary. The Quiristers then used the building for daily Latin prayers. The upper room was

* Under this marble is buried / Thomas Welsted / whom death by the blow of a stone / laid low. In this school / he was first, nor / as we hope in heaven is he last / where instead of Oxford he went up / on 13 January / in the year of Our Lord 1676 and in the 18th year of his life.

St. Michael's

briefly a granary, before a seventeenth century Warden turned it into a book store, and the lower chapel into a Fellows' library, but one of ever-decreasing activity. The arrival of the great influx of Commoners in the 1860's led to a revival of Chantry's original religious use, for the school numbers became too great to be accommodated within Chapel alone. From the 1870's to the 1960's, Chantry served as a sort of 'junior chapel' until it too was outgrown by ever-increasing numbers, and the junior boys decamped, spiritually at least, to St Michael's on the west side of Kingsgate Street. In the meantime, the upper room – delightfully light, remote and secluded – had a brief run as the school's Art Room, before art too burst its bounds and went elsewhere, as we shall see later. It now houses the school's collection of *Wiccamica* – books, papers and other ephemera, some dating back to the seventeenth century, and miscellaneous artefacts like the Brickdale Triptych and Wavell's sword .

Chantry now holds occasional services, and indeed has enjoyed a recent religious renaissance of a different hue, as the venue for occasional Roman Catholic services. It has a piano, for the use of the many musical Scholars, and will shortly have its own organ. But otherwise it has generally returned to the state of peaceful solitude in which we have found it, and which we will now leave for the greater hurly-burly of the schoolroom.

Flint Court

7 SCHOOL AND SCHOOLROOMS

Like the interior of Chapel, the schoolrooms of the College have evolved through distinct phases over the last six centuries.

On the way from Chamber Court to Cloisters, we passed through Seventh Chamber Passage. We shall now return there, and look inside Seventh Chamber itself. The passage was carved out of the original Chamber in 1687 to facilitate access to the new School: the original three-windowed room would have been rather lighter as well as larger. The Chamber itself is arguably the oldest schoolroom in England, and the only one which has been in continuous use since the fourteenth century. Substantially refurbished and modernized thanks to the College's 1973 Development Appeal, the interior now looks less forbidding and spartan than it evidently appeared to Radclyffe in 1846: some concessions have been made to the twentieth century, and indeed the visitor also has to banish from his imagination the new mezzanine floor filling the northern half of the Chamber. Nevertheless, some of the flavour of the original still endures, and this, for nearly three hundred years, was the schoolroom for the seventy Scholars.

A Flint Court Div Room

School

Then, in 1687, came School, arguably at that time the greatest single act of modernization and improvement within the College since the Foundation. We can see School, directly opposite, through the windows of Seventh Chamber, and it will take us but a moment to return to Seventh Chamber Passage and then walk across School Court to admire the elegance of its north-facing exterior. The south-facing exterior, by contrast, is virtually devoid of ornamentation, because at the end of the seventeenth century there was none of today's pedestrian traffic in Meads for whose visual gratification the architect would otherwise have had to cater. Who was the architect? As we have already noticed when passing the Barracks and Wolvesey, Wren himself was engaged elsewhere in Winchester at the time that School was built, and the grace and elegance of the building strongly suggest his influence, if not his work. Alas, however, there is no evidence to support attributing School to his actual design, and it has to be content with the (lower case) label "school of Wren".

This delightfully proportioned and decorated building was built at a cost of £2,600, of which more than half was contributed by Warden Nicholas himself (although before we become too admiring of his munificence, we should bear in mind that he, like all Wardens and Fellows of the post-Reformation and pre-Victorian College, "did very nicely indeed" out of the revenues of the Foundation). The same Warden Nicholas also commissioned the Pierce panelling in Chapel which we will meet later in this stroll, notwithstanding its disappearance from Chapel in the nineteenth century. Today School is used largely for concerts, talks and social functions, and also at the beginning of the school year for the ceremonial induction of the new Scholars and at the end of the year for academic prize-giving. In the late nineteenth century, before the advent of the present Music School, this was the College's only large auditorium apart from Chapel, and late Victorian photographs of the interior show a raised stage at the east end, and even an organ.

School's original purpose, however, was as ' the schoolroom' of the College, and it was used for that purpose for nearly two centuries, with different classes all hugger-mugger. We can still see the Headmaster's 'throne' in the south-west corner, from which today's Warden conducts the admission of new Scholars, and the Second Master's seat opposite. The twentieth century headmasters (and, in one case, a remarkably colourful necktie) look down from their portraits on the walls. On the wall at the east end is the *Tabula Legum Paedagogicarum,* the painted panel of school rules, originating from the Foundation and seen here as revised by Warden Huntingford at the end of the eighteenth century; virtually all of the rules have long since fallen into desuetude, but they end on a nicely enduring modern note (which perhaps might at least subconsciously have influenced the United States President, Bill Clinton, had he but known it) – … *tertia vice expellimus*, which may loosely be construed as "three strikes and you're out". At the west end is the "*Aut Disce*" board, displaying the perfect Latin hexametrical exhortation *aut disce aut discede – manet sors tertia caedi** (or in the more prosaic modern vernacular "learn, leave or be licked"). Above the entrance outside and above the fireplace within, the Founder's statue and portrait survey all.

Not the least of the reasons for building School was the pressure of numbers on the much smaller space in Seventh Chamber. We have in this stroll met constant reminders of the original seventy Scholars, but from the very earliest times their numbers were swollen, for teaching purposes, by 'Commoners' – young gentlemen who were billeted in buildings, now long demolished, on the west side of the medieval buildings, and from whose fee-paying parents successive Headmasters earned a substantial additional stipend. With the reforms of the 1860's came a large increase in the number of Commoners – and indeed, by the end of the 1860's, the establishment of nine of the ten modern Commoner houses. Those numbers necessitated the abandonment of School and the construction of the present 'div rooms' grouped round Flint Court. These are the red brick buildings away to our left as we come out of School, the main 'h' shaped structure being the work of Butterfield at the end of the 1860's, substantially on the site of the old barrack-like block where the boarding Commoners had previously lived. "Mr Butterfield" said the Warden of the day, "you have made a silk purse out of a sow's ear". Butterfield's work provided 18 new classrooms, with a further eight being added at the south-west corner of Flint Court in 1883.

* Either learn, or leave: there remains the third option, to be beaten.

Seventh Chamber

School

Flint Court

This third phase of the College's schoolroom evolution still endures and provides today's core teaching facilities. On a working day, we may stand quite alone in the middle of Flint Court for most of an hour, and then for five minutes between lessons Flint Court is a hive of activity, as several hundred boys move from the feet of one master or, today, mistress to another, before our solitude is restored. But these are not the only current classrooms: we will not visit all the outstations, but could hardly ignore altogether the Sciences – a late arrival in terms of the College's history, an avant garde novelty by contemporary standards. We walk down the flagstone path on the west side of Meads, past a series of buildings to which we shall be returning very shortly, and through Ridding Gate in the south-west corner into New Field. To our right is Science School, a neo-classical block built in the first rush of twentieth century Wykehamist development in 1905. With it came a flourishing of scientific study at Winchester; and at much the same time history, modern languages and other non-Classical subjects blossomed. It is perhaps hard for today's visitor to comprehend, surveying a polymathic school with only bare traces of Latin and Greek still clinging to the curriculum, how Winchester was an entirely Classics-oriented school until the end of the nineteenth century.

We shall shortly go and look at some other buildings reflecting modernity and diversification. But first we must go to war.

Eccles Room

8 WAR CLOISTERS

We have already seen the College's Crimean War Memorial, on our way through the ante-chapel into Chapel itself, with the names of the thirteen Wykehamists who died in the Crimean War of 1854–6. Had we passed through Commoner Gate when contemplating our choice of entrance into the College, we would have been able to count the thirty-two names on the memorial to the dead of the South African War of 1899–1902 and, the eleven post-War dead in conflicts from Palestine in 1948 to Malaya in 1955, besides also seeing the sad memorials to the two Wykehamists killed by the IRA during the recent 'Troubles'. But none of those memorials to lesser conflicts distant in time or place, or both, prepares the visitor for the sheer numbers of dead commemorated in War Cloisters.

During World War I, over 2,200 Wykehamists saw active service. None rose above the rank of Lieutenant General, but their combined gallantry awards included 214 DSO's, 320 MC's and 4 Victoria Crosses. In World War II, in addition to Wavell on land, two Wykehamist airmen reached the zenith of their service – Portal as Chief of the Air Staff for most of the war, and Dowding at the head of Fighter Command in 1940. Indeed, the shamefully under-honoured Dowding could be said to have been the ultimate single saviour of Britain in that momentous year. The number called to the Colours was smaller, but Wykehamists still won 26 DSO's, 18 MC's, 26 DSC's and 29 DFC's. But at what a cost. 500 Wykehamists fell in the First War, or well over ten per cent of the entire Wykehamist body, and they were followed only a generation later by 270 dead in the Second War. For a school which had entered the twentieth century with few military aspirations – Dr Fearon's letter to Colonel Wavell was entirely in keeping with the contemporary outlook – Winchester has subsequently paid its military dues with a vengeance.

Well before the First War ended, discussions were taking place about a suitable memorial to the fallen, even to the extent of a remarkable Old Wykehamist dinner held in Amiens on the eve of the battle of Cambrai in November 1917, attended by the then Headmaster Dr Rendall in order to ascertain the views of – in one sense – the very men who might be commemorated. Both then and in all other discussions, it was agreed that the first priority was the provision of funds for the education of the sons of Wykehamists killed; and indeed ample provision for that purpose was duly made, even if the average age of the dead meant that very few left sons needing this benefit. But what was to be the physical embodiment of the College's memorial to the dead? Schemes grandiose and utilitarian were proposed: to move School bodily from the dominating proximity of the mediaeval buildings; to build a new concert and lecture

War Cloisters looking towards Meads

Gates to War Cloisters

Commoner Gate

hall, or a central dining hall; to fund much wider access to the College by those whose parents could not afford the fees; and others besides.

In the end, the decision was made to build a purely commemorative and non-utilitarian edifice, and the result was War Cloisters, built at a cost of £65,000 and dedicated in 1924, all within six years after the end of the War. The architect was Sir Herbert Baker, the co-designer of the British Raj's lasting monument, New Delhi, and architect also of numerous other war memorials, both in England and on the Western Front. We shall be meeting Baker again when we come to Moberly Library. The designer of the garden in the middle of War Cloisters was Gertrude Jekyll.

War Cloisters, as one of the College's distinguished chroniclers has observed, are complementary to Wykeham's Cloisters but do not challenge them; the materials and dimensions are approximately the same, but not the purpose or style. Unlike the unfrequented cul-de-sac of Cloisters, War Cloisters are a main thoroughfare: the vast majority of the 600 Commoners have to pass through them every day, between their houses and the classrooms. Yet at the same time War Cloisters share with Cloisters a serenity, a sanctity even, which is quite unaffected by the constant passage of pedestrian traffic.

Pevsner describes War Cloisters as one of Baker's best buildings, and it is hard to disagree with the notion that this is one of the most beautiful war memorials in England. Largely flint, dressed with cut stone, it is very simple, but also almost unbearably poignant. Follow the stone slabs round the outer walls, with the names engraved of the First War dead and their regiments and battlefields; and then begin all over again with the inner pillars, and the names of the Second War dead, in whose honour War Cloisters were reconsecrated in 1948. The visitor cannot fail to be moved.

In the recess half way along the west side is a bronze bust of Dowding, by David Wynne in 1974, a fine likeness of that very great man. Directly opposite on the east side, the view into Meads through the ornamental gates topped by angels originally made by one Art Master, Professor Gleadowe (who also designed the Sword of Stalingrad, the nation's wartime gift to the Soviet Union in honour of the sacrifice and victory at Stalingrad), and much more recently replaced (the originals having been stolen) by another, Arthur Morgan, is one of the prettiest of Wykehamical sylvan scenes.

In the largely unvisited north-west corner of War Cloisters is a blocked doorway. An early design for New Hall contemplated its siting immediately to the north of War Cloisters, with this doorway providing one means of access. Fortunately for the tenants of the considerable number of gardens on the east side of Kingsgate Street which would have been devoured by the new building, the Governing Body had prudent cold feet and decided to opt instead for the south side of the Warden's Garden, which we will be visiting shortly.

Arts Centre

9 MUSES AND WHITE ELEPHANTS

Let us now leave the peaceful beauty of War Cloisters, and visit the several Wykehamical homes of the artistic, musical and dramatic Muses.

Art, in terms of education in the appreciation and creation of the visual arts, was something of a late arrival at the College. As recently as the 1920's, Kenneth Clark received a report in his last year that said that he "should keep art as a hobby, and retain a sense of proportion". Clark's appreciation of Civilization might be said to have emerged and flourished in spite of Winchester, rather than thanks to it.

The College's first purpose-built art schoolroom was Museum, by Basil Champney, which stands on the west side of Meads immediately to the south of War Cloisters. Museum was the not entirely happy compromise which was eventually agreed by the ponderously large committee appointed by the Warden and Fellows to determine an appropriate edifice to mark the College's quincentenary. It was built in 1897, and so coincided rather more accurately with Queen Victoria's Diamond Jubilee than with any plausible date for the quincentenary: indeed, Queen Victoria and the Founder are the subjects of the two statues at either end of the upper facade. Pevsner describes Museum as "curiously Baroque", but demonstrates a certain sympathy with it by wondering whether the double-columned recessed loggia may have inspired Baker's double columns in War Cloisters.

Despite some distinguished Art Masters – Gleadowe, Sthyr, and in particular Grahame Drew, who inspired a devoted following over his twenty year tenure of the post – the teaching of art in Museum always remained a minor activity in the Winchester curriculum: the resources required for a large-scale art school simply were not there. At one early stage, the teaching of drawing withdrew to the upstairs room above Chantry – a delightful room, full of natural light, but with impractical access by a narrow spiral staircase, and after a brief stay the drawing Muse returned to Museum. The long gallery on the upper floor of Museum used to display worthy but less than inspiring exhibits, when not hosting once a year prospective Scholars sitting the Election Exam, or miscellaneous social functions.

More recently, thanks to the energetic inspiration of John Thorn, then the Headmaster, and the dedicated efforts of Arthur Morgan, for 25 years the Art Master, "art" has moved out of Museum altogether; the principal accommodation – the upstairs gallery – has subsequently been turned into the Dons' Common Room. It is difficult to disagree with the description of Museum by the most recent of the College's distinguished chroniclers as "an expensive neo-Brunelleschian monument

Sculpting in Art Centre

to the dangers of unplanned development: a mistake, well-intentioned, but a mistake nonetheless". Or, if you like, a white elephant.

Separated from Museum by College Sick House is Winchester's other spectacular Victorian white elephant, the former Sanatorium, now the home of "art". Built as a result of general concerns in the 1870's and 1880's about health and hygiene, with two operating theatres and capacity for over thirty in-patients, Sanatorium was never (fortunately) fully used. Through a glass very darkly, the building might suggest a Ruritanian castle, with its steep roofs and ludicrous corner turrets – added afterwards, as school lore had it, to house the plumbing which the architect originally forgot.

What was to be done with this redundant Victorian pachyderm? One mooted possibility was the complete demolition of the building, and its replacement with a new boarding house (even the most recent of the ten Commoner boarding houses is

Museum

now nearly a hundred years old), but the Victorian Society threw a fit, the quart of the new house would not fit into the pint pot of the site, and the College's finances were stretched at the time with other pressing expenditure on the fabric of the Foundation. To the Works Bursar falls the Sisyphean lot of the upkeep of the buildings: Chapel, School and New Hall all seem to be on roughly forty year cycles for major restoration work, and the fabric of the College overall is as ceaselessly demanding as the Forth Bridge.

The answer was provided by Ted Cullinan, of Edward Cullinan Architects, who were also responsible for the conversion of the old gymnasium into the QEII Theatre. The unused Sanatorium was transformed into a vibrant Arts Centre, full of activity and natural light in place of the previous sepulchral gloom, and with the two Ruritanian 'keeps' connected by an uncompromisingly modern bridge, with its hint of

Jazz quartet

Burgundian rooftops. On the lawn between Arts Centre and Kingsgate Street, set discreetly in the grass, is Arthur Morgan's maze, which has yet to be solved without its creator's help.

Music, too, has been in some ways a late starter at the College. Although the sixteen Quiristers have been there since the Foundation, the school established a proper orchestra only after the first five hundred years of its life, and a Music School only in the first five years of the twentieth century. Before then School, having been abandoned as the schoolroom after the building of Butterfield's present 'div rooms', had briefly been the principal music centre, with the stage and organ whose shades we noticed earlier. There was music, but it was not a mainstream activity.

But with the arrival of the Edwardian Music School, and then successive Directors of Music of the distinction of Dyson, Watson, Havergal, Cowan, another Watson and Keith Pusey, the teaching and playing of music in the school has flourished. A substantial majority of the boys now play one or more musical instruments. Music has long since lost its status as Cinderella to outdoor sports, and

Academy Orchestra

New Hall, Pierce Panelling

Wykehamists have achieved great success in the musical world, both during and after their time in the school. In one respect, music was the victim of its own success in the school, because the pressures on the limited facilities in the original Music School were becoming intolerable. Happily another of the College's Development Appeals has permitted the construction of the very successful twenty-first century extension to Music School, which has earned its designers, NVB Architects, a City of Winchester City Trust Design Award, and has doubled the music teaching space. More space and better facilities have also permitted more music in common with the wider Winchester community, which in turn reinforces the civic integration of the College.

The musical and dramatic Muses also lead us back to the east side of the College, beyond Meads and through Non Licet Gate, to the austerely plain building which we passed at the outset of our stroll. This is New Hall – not an inspired name, perhaps, but if it is good enough for Wykeham's College at Oxford, it will do just as well here too. New Hall, in conception, had several purposes. When it was built, it could just about seat the entire school, although the number of boys has continued to grow so that, once again, the only building in Winchester with that capacity is the Cathedral (hence the uniqueness of the '*Ad Portas*' ceremony mentioned in Chapter 5). It also gave the school a 'proper' theatre and concert hall: 'proper', in terms of a decent-sized auditorium and stage, when none had existed before, but largely deficient in backstage and technical attributes, and the bulk of Winchester's drama now happens in the QEII Theatre. Major productions still gravitate towards New Hall, with its greater seating capacity, but it is bedevilled by acoustics which, while fine for music and even for opera, are poor for speech and for drama.

New Hall's finest and most famous production was arguably, but also appropriately, its first: the week-long run of '*The Masque*' in July 1961, a dramatic account of the entire history of the College, written to celebrate the opening of the Hall, playing to a packed house every night, displaying the very best of Wykehamical style and wit, and attracting the critical approbation of the national and even foreign newspapers. Indeed, not the least of New Hall's purposes is celebrated, most appropriately, in the final scene of '*The Masque*', immediately before the Epilogue, the players being six figures bearing sandwich-boards representing the 1682 Pierce panelling which had been removed from Chapel in the 1870's. With, as the players sing, "matchless generosity", Sir George Cooper, at whose home in Hursley Park the panelling had resided in the meantime, gave it back to the College in 1956. Thanks to the ingenuity of the architect, Peter Shepheard, and further grants from the Dulverton and Pilgrim Trusts, the panelling was installed in New Hall.

King Lear in QEII Theatre

We recross Meads once again in order to visit the last building on our tour of the Muses, but before doing so let us stop briefly just inside and to the left of Non Licet Gate, and peer at a piece of perspex fixed to the wall at chest height. We look more closely, and can just discern "A. Trollope" scratched into the wall: to the best of anyone's knowledge, it is genuinely the author's own graffito. Then across Meads, passing between Museum and College Sick House, and into the QEII Theatre. Until the late 1960's, this was the old Victorian gymnasium, rendered briefly redundant by the opening of the present PE Centre on the far side of Kingsgate Park, but now enjoying since the early 1970's a far more useful and pleasurable second life – again thanks to the inspiration of John Thorn – as a small theatre. It does not have the capacity of New Hall, but otherwise has much better facilities, particularly for the profusion of House plays which its existence has spawned; it also has an intimacy, a rapport between audience and stage, which New Hall lacks. Perhaps most importantly, its sole purpose is as a theatre, and it does not suffer New Hall's multi-tasked disadvantages. Its name, of course, is taken from The Queen herself, who opened Ted Cullinan's enhanced theatre on 19 May 1982 in the course of her memorable sescentennial visit.

We began this Chapter in search of Muses, and encountered at least the shades of several white elephants. It is a happy tribute to the imagination, effort and expense which have been devoted over the years to the constant recycling and improvement of the fabric of the Foundation that there are so few elephant bones on the ground today.

Non Licet Gate. Anthony Trollope carved his name in the wall immediately to the left of the stairs

Fellows' Library

10 LIBRARIES AND LODGINGS

There are two buildings in Outer Court with unassuming exteriors which we neglected in our original passage from Outer Gate to Chamber Court.

If we stand by the small clump of trees against the wall which divides Outer Court and screens the former stables on the west side, we are – according to the geography of the school – in Paradise, although it has to be said that the name comes from the Greek word παραδεισος, meaning an enclosed park or pleasure ground, rather than from any more celestial aspirations. Whether it is Paradise Lost or Regained – the other half of that pair being the scrubby clump on the little island in Logie (the stream running past the east side of the mediaeval buildings) on the north side of College Street – is one of those timeless Wykehamical uncertainties, although it is indisputable that the small garden on the west side of the screening wall forms part of Arcadia, being a land of rural bliss under the trees of Paradise.

On the east side of that screening wall is a lion's head, said to be the emblem of St Elizabeth of Hungary and to have been fixed there in her honour as a relic of the College (or more accurately, minor religious establishment) bearing her name which was expropriated and dissolved by Henry VIII in 1539 and demolished in 1547. We shall meet the stones, at least, of St Elizabeth College in the next Chapter.

The first of the two buildings which we have come to see is the one fronting on to the east side of Outer Court. Its dour knapped flint exterior, by G S Repton in 1831, conceals a much earlier and more pleasing residence, the Warden's Lodgings. Wykeham's original Warden and his successors for the first 200 years of the College's existence lived 'above the shop', as it were, in rooms above Middle Gate which Wykeham considered quite sufficient for an unmarried cleric. During that time, Outer Court ran the full length of the north range of Chamber Court; the east end was bordered by the Slaughterhouse, Bakehouse and Granaries, just as today's surviving west end is bordered by the old Brewery and Stables. But with the sixteenth century and the Reformation came the first married Warden, and grandeur and good living at the Foundation's much abused expense which only came to an end with the death of the last of the Wardens appointed before the great Victorian reforms, Warden Lee, in 1901.

Warden Harman built the new Lodgings in 1597. They were enlarged by Warden Nicholas, whom we have already met in School, and again by the first Warden Lee in the eighteenth century, and the Repton façade was added at the end of Warden Huntingford's long tenure in the early nineteenth century, with the Fellows' Library on the first floor. An elegant and capacious dining room looks out over College Street, and can seat twenty-four at a squeeze. An equally distinguished panelled sitting-room surveys the Warden's Garden, and is adorned with a rotating selection of watercolours by Turner and Brabazon among others, from the three substantial collections of watercolours which the College received from munificent benefactors during the later part of the twentieth century. A further selection is on display from time to time in the Arts Centre. A number of bedrooms and bathrooms add to the feeling of a large and comfortable, and grand but not too grand, country house. If all that begins to sound like a hotel brochure, it is true that the College now lets the Lodgings for private functions, and a very elegant venue they make.

Two rooms in the Lodgings are likely to escape us, even if we are paying guests for the weekend: we would probably need the presence of the Warden himself, as our host, to gain access. The first is the Fellows' Library, on the first floor above Repton's front door, overlooking Outer Court. Zealously guarded by the Fellows' Librarian, the Library is rarely seen, except on the occasional visits of the Warden and Fellows. This is a pity, since the Library is one of the most beautiful rooms in the College. On the second floor, a large well-proportioned panelled room looking out over College Street – currently the office of the Archivist – is the Posers' Room: the name refers not to

Outer Court

Warden's Lodgings

modern thespians, but to the two Fellows of New College who came down to Winchester at the end of every year for the annual scholarship exams *ad Oxon*.

Moberly Library (named in honour of Dr Moberly, one of the great Victorian Headmasters) started life in 1870, in what are now the 'div rooms' above the cross-piece of the Butterfield buildings, at the north end of Flint Court. In 1934, the Library was moved to Sir Herbert Baker's second distinguished contribution to the College's architecture – the conversion of the old Brewery, backing onto College Street on the west side of Outer Gate. The original conversion has subsequently been augmented by the munificence of three Wykehamist families: the Eccles Room, on the ground floor of the old Brewery, now contains the College's rarer literary treasures (as distinct from the *Wiccamica* now housed above Chantry), and the Makins and Blackwell Rooms on the first floor of the old Headmaster's House have both substantially extended the Library's floor and shelf space and averted another white elephant. The old Headmaster's House, also designed by Repton in 1839, at the instigation of Dr Moberly himself, was a lugubrious and increasingly impractical building for a late twentieth century family home, and John Thorn took the sensible step of moving out. The Headmaster now resides in Kingsgate Street, opposite Commoner Gate, leaving only the Headmaster's Study and his

Moberly Library staircase with carved owl on newel post

Moberly Library and Dominions Clock

immediate supporting staff on the ground floor of his former official residence. A bridge over Moberly Gate now connects the Makins Room to the old Brewery.

Baker succeeded in preserving the structure and appearance of the mediaeval brewery, while at the same time creating within it a peaceful, practical and visually pleasing contemporary library, with its characteristic smell of oak and books and wax. At the east end there are two particular curios: the delightfully carved owl at the bottom of the oak banister; and on the east wall itself the Dominions Clock. This is a fearsomely complicated timepiece, presented by Baker to the school in 1936. The clock consists of an inner dial which is a 12-hour clock with a second hand in stainless steel, in addition to gilt hour and minute hands. Round this is a dial which revolves once in 24 hours, the 24 numerals of the hours being carved on the stone surround. On this outer dial are the symbols showing the time at Greenwich and the standard times or time-zones of the Dominions and some of the greater Dependencies, as they existed in 1936. The sun and moon emblems were modelled by Sir Charles Wheeler RA, and the Greek inscription was composed by Dr Rendall –

ΣΩΜΑ ΜΕΝ ᾽ΑΝΘΡΩΠΟΙ
ΨΥΧΗΝ ΔΕ ΜΟΙ ΩΠΑΣΕΝ ᾽ΑΙΘΗΡ *

*   Mankind gave me a body
      Heaven gave me a soul

11 GARDENS AND GREENERY

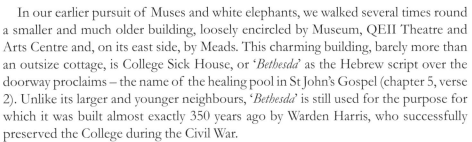

In our earlier pursuit of Muses and white elephants, we walked several times round a smaller and much older building, loosely encircled by Museum, QEII Theatre and Arts Centre and, on its east side, by Meads. This charming building, barely more than an outsize cottage, is College Sick House, or '*Bethesda*' as the Hebrew script over the doorway proclaims – the name of the healing pool in St John's Gospel (chapter 5, verse 2). Unlike its larger and younger neighbours, '*Bethesda*' is still used for the purpose for which it was built almost exactly 350 years ago by Warden Harris, who successfully preserved the College during the Civil War.

To the immediate south of Sick House is the Apothecary's Garden. If the low brick wall surrounding it is too high for the viewer, a raised platform is conveniently provided behind the south wall to facilitate viewing the garden. Sick House has always had its appurtenant garden, but the present horticultural design and content are the work of Rachel Bebb, herself a Wykehamist wife, with the active support and encouragement of Lady Morse, the wife of the then Warden, and principally funded by the Dinwiddy family, in memory of John Dinwiddy. As Rachel Bebb has written, it is tempting to think that the original apothecary in residence would have grown medicinal plants, perhaps encouraged by the Physic Gardens of Oxford or Chelsea, or even the fine garden at New College. The present garden is a recreation not of the seventeenth century actuality, which has long since been lost in the mists of time, but rather of plausibility: the plants in the recreated garden were known in the seventeenth century, some being included for their ornamental value, but many also for their traditional medicinal properties. The arbour is based on a design on an embroidered box belonging to the Embroiderers' Guild and made at much the same time as Sick House was built. The seats were specially made for the recreated garden, bearing an amalgam of the arms of the College and the arms of the Society of Apothecaries (unicorn horns were believed to be an antidote to poison), whose Master opened the completed garden in 1992.

Sick House was built on part of the meadow acquired by the College a century earlier. After Henry VIII's expropriation of the former Carmelite Friary, the College exchanged some existing Thames-side landholdings for the meadow, the larger part of which is now incorporated in Meads. Before then, and for the first 150 years of the College's life, Meads was considerably smaller than the playing field which we see today, and its use as a playing field at all only dates from the nineteenth century. Much of the wall around Meads was built in 1548 from the stones of the former St Elizabeth

Moberly Court

College – a reminder of the similar fate which this College so narrowly escaped at that time. In the middle of Meads is the 2nd XI cricket square: as with the St Lawrence County Ground at Canterbury until the sad demise of its offending tree in 2004, two large plane trees standing well within the boundary require 'local rules', being treated as non-scoring passive fielders. It is the trees, as much as any other aspect, which give Meads its particular charm: a large open space, reduced to more intimate proportions by the profusion of majestic trees, achieving a perfect balance between impressions of protectiveness and openness, while always fostering a sense of informality and light.

The great expansion of the school's playing fields was the work of Dr Ridding, the Second Founder. Passing once again through Ridding Gate in the south-west corner of Meads, we are on New Field, a relatively vast open space stretching right down to Garnier Road. At Ridding's sole initiative and expense, most of New Field was reclaimed from unusable bog in less than two years. The southern section – roughly speaking, Bull's Drove, from Hunter Tent down to Garnier Road itself – had to await the twentieth century, as did Kingsgate Park and Palmer Field. Nevertheless, by 1870 the first 'Eton Match' could be played (and won) on New Field, which was described by Lady Laura Ridding, Ridding's second wife and the daughter of the Victorian Lord Chancellor the Earl of Selborne, as "the crowning beauty of Winchester College"; and it is hard not to share Firth's difficulty in imagining a lovelier setting for cricket.

Even with Ridding's great expansion on New Field, Winchester is not blessed with the rolling acres of, say, Eton or Charterhouse, and most of the playing fields have to double up and earn their keep in different guises throughout the year. Every year the tiny groundstaff – the Head Groundsman and his permanent team of four – manage horticultural miracles, as the muddy swamp of a Winchester College Football 'canvas' has to be turned into a cricket outfield or a running track, or a football pitch into tennis courts.

The College's various gardens are maintained by an equally small band of four gardeners. We have already seen the two sets of Cloisters which they maintain, and Arcadia and the Apothecary's Garden, not to mention also the gardens of the Commoner houses, which we are not visiting. Their largest charge, however, we shall visit: we have already seen a glimpse of the Warden's Garden from Cloisters' Bell Gate, and a more panoramic view from the Warden's first-floor drawing room. Large, secluded, private; well-bordered on its north and east sides; a wide expanse of immaculately maintained lawn bordering Logie, the stream; and immediately beyond it the Lodgings, the eastern exterior of Chamber Court, and the east window of Chapel. Stand in the right place, ignoring New Hall, and the view has been pretty much the same for the best part of four hundred years.

Arts Centre and Ridding Gate

We may have the Warden's Garden to ourselves. We may share it with a few Scholars and a game of croquet: the Garden's eponymous landlord is rarely in residence, and generously makes his domain available to more immediate users. We may hear the *tunk* of tennis balls from the courts in the south-east corner which, to the regret of recent Headmasters, have replaced the asparagus beds in the former vegetable garden. We may find the Friends of Winchester College (largely local, enthusiastic, and extremely munificent supporters of the College and its activities) having a summer party. We may even be present on the last evening of Cloister Time, the summer term, when 'Domum' is sung.

'Domum' (for this purpose, with a long 'o', notwithstanding the correct short 'o' in the Latin '*domus*', meaning a house or home) is Winchester's school song. Uniquely, certainly among the great English public schools, 'Domum' extols not the virtues and victories of the College, but the joys of the singers' imminent departure homewards. Again, its origins are lost in Wykehamical mists of time. One root is the cry of 'Domum' which mustered the Scholars playing on top of St Catherine's Hill (or 'Hills'), before their return journey to the College: the same Headmaster, Christopher Johnson, who at least apocryphally gave us the Trusty Servant's verse in the sixteenth century, also encouraged the boys to take exercise on Hills, a practice which died in the mid-nineteenth century, but was subsequently revived as a symbolic tradition which we shall

meet in the last Chapter. Another, more plausible root traces 'Domum' to the plague of 1666 (which we met briefly in Chapter 2), when the school was dispersed elsewhere, and in particular to Crawley, where it may have been composed by a group of temporarily exiled Scholars; the words were re-set to music by John Reading, the College organist from 1681 – 1692. The first line of the fifth verse "*Heus! Rogere, fer caballos*", which has sent many a new boy searching vainly for obscure parts of the verb *rogare* (to ask), in fact simply means "Ho! Roger, fetch the horses", and helpfully dates the composition by the reference to Roger Oades, the College odd-job man and ostler of the time. We shall leave the Warden's Garden to the refrain of 'Domum' –

Domum, Domum, dulce Domum,
Dulce Domum resonemus

College Sick House and Apothecary's Garden

Queen Inn

12 VICTUALLING AND RETAILING

It is time for the refreshments which were promised many chapters ago.

Kingsgate today permits only pedestrian and bicycle traffic. Since 1990, two discreet but solid stone bollards either side of the archway have barred the motor traffic which used to turn the Kingsgate junction into Winchester's worst permanent traffic jam. The two bollards are also a silent tribute to the late Graeme Jameson, who was a leading campaigner for them, and to whom thanks are therefore due for the restoration of relative freedom from the motor car on the College side of Kingsgate.

It is Graeme Jameson's other and larger legacy which is of more immediate interest to us, and this is The Wykeham Arms on the corner of Canon Street. A public house for 250 years, The Wykeham Arms achieved widespread plaudits and renown under his direction, and its standards continue under the management of Kate and Peter Miller, receiving regular high praise in the Good Food, Pub and Hotel Guides, among others. We may lunch or dine there, or just graze throughout the day, surrounded by a large quantity of Wykehamical and Winchester prints and pictures. We may also stay the night, in comfortable rooms both upstairs and across the other side of Kingsgate Street, in the related 'St George'.

Kingsgate

If we are minded to go back 'up town', we may try Winchester's other highly praised hotel and restaurant. A short walk up St Swithun Street or Canon Street, and then right into Southgate Street, past the former Green Jackets Chapel (now a cinema, and possibly the only one in England with a church cross over its main entrance) and the Royal Hampshire Regiment Museum in Searle House, brings us to a large elegant early Georgian façade, dating back to 1715, formerly housing the Southgate Hotel, and now much rejuvenated by its present incarnation as the Hotel and Bistro du Vin (which was the first of the several hotels of that name now dotted round England).

Alternatively, if we would like a head start before climbing St Catherine's Hill, another walk down Kingsgate Street and its continuation as Kingsgate Road, past Altham Gates, brings us to The Queen Inn, just before the Norman Road junction. Less *Wiccamica*, and a shorter wine list, but useful car parking and an ample garden; less of a hotel-restaurant, more of an ordinary but pleasant pub.

Those who have taken the Hotel du Vin option will find plenty of retail opportunities in the commercial heart of the town, but the south side of Kingsgate is not without its shopping possibilities. We have already noted the print shop under Kingsgate itself. Directly opposite the archway, on the corner of College and Kingsgate Streets, is Cornflowers, the College's own giftshop, selling a wide array of

Hotel du Vin

Cornflowers and The Wykeham Arms

Wykehamical memorabilia and other useful or pretty presents. Just beyond the 'St George' annex of The Wykeham Arms is 'Kingsgate Wines and Provisions' – sadly no longer a Post Office, but still a comprehensively stocked 'village store', with the bonus of being a fine wine shop.

The oldest and most famous of the local shops is Wells, the College bookshop, although it now serves a substantially wider clientele than merely the College, being a fine new and second-hand general bookshop. The name Wells first became associated with the premises in 1834, when Joseph Wells was apprenticed to James Robbins, who had owned since 1806 the bookselling, bookbinding and printing business then carried on in College Street. It is not unduly fanciful to imagine that Jane Austen, who lived her last few months before her death in 1817 at Number 8 College Street, only three doors to the east, would have been among Robbins' customers. Before Robbins, Thomas and John Burdon had been trading as booksellers in College Street since as early as 1757, and the College's own records include a bill from the Burdons' predecessor in business, Ambrose Holloway, from 1729.

When Robbins died in 1844 and the business was bought by David Nutt, a London bookseller (not least at the instigation of Dr Moberly, the then Headmaster, who was anxious that the business should continue), Wells ran the shop in Winchester, while

The Wykeham Arms

Nutt stayed in London. After a brief spell in partnership with Nutt until Nutt's death in 1865, Joseph Wells began in 1866 the Wells family's exclusive association with the shop which continued until, after four generations, the family sold the premises and business in 1983. The premises were bought by the College, and the business has continued since then under the management of Matthew Huntley.

Both the elegant mahogany and glass shopfront and the continuing trading name 'P & G Wells' date from the second generation and the brief period around the end of the nineteenth century when Joseph's sons, Philip and George, ran the business in partnership. In Joseph's time, the premises had more the look of a house than a shop, with shuttered windows on the ground floor and an imposing front door framed by columns and a pediment. Shortly after George's death, Philip's daughter Margaret joined her father in the shop in 1908, at the age of 17, beginning a remarkable association with the business which lasted 71 years until her retirement in 1979 at the age of 88.

Those of a more idle disposition may happily spend the rest of the day in Wells, or in any other of these shops and watering holes. For the more energetic, there remains the final and most strenuous part of this stroll, to St Catherine's Hill and St Cross.

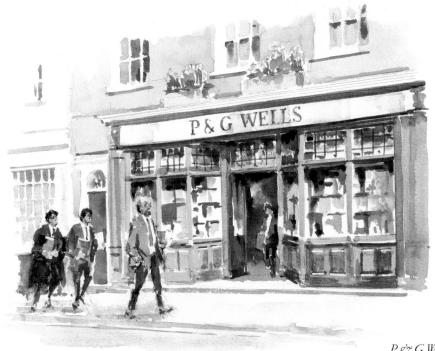

P & G Wells

St. Cross from the river

13 ST CATHERINE'S HILL AND
ST CROSS – ENVOI

At various times during our stroll we have looked out over the playing fields and water-meadows to the hill in the middle distance. This is St Catherine's Hill, or just 'Hills' to Wykehamists – a 300 foot high former Iron Age fort. On a fine day it will amply repay a climb, with its splendid panorama of Winchester and the surrounding countryside.

If we are taking advantage of a head start at The Queen Inn, we cross New Field and the foot-bridge over Logie, and then follow the river down to Garnier Road. Turning east, we reach Tunbridge, which takes us over New Barge. Over the last hundred years or so, this unpromising-looking former canal has spawned a number of successful Wykehamist oarsmen and rowing IV's and VIII's. It was first cut by Bishop Godfrey de Lucy as long ago as the twelfth century, as a trading waterway connecting Winchester to what is now Southampton. Its use subsided during the Middle Ages, revived in the seventeenth and eighteenth centuries, but ceased absolutely in about 1870. Now the only remaining navigable stretch is the three-quarters of a mile or so over which the College has, it seems, exclusive aquatic rights. We follow its towpath to the bottom of the navigable stretch. In doing so, we also see a neat little self-contained exemplar of English transport history since the Industrial Revolution. Immediately to the east of the redundant canal are the remains of the embankment of Winchester's former second (Great Western) railway line, with its station in Chesil Street at the lower, east end of the town: the line succumbed to Dr Beeching's axe many years ago. On the other side of the railway line was the old Winchester by-pass, an early (1930's) dual carriageway: it too, at least along the stretch of our walk, has disappeared completely, having been effectively supplanted by the extended M3 motorway, running the other side of Hills. The effect has been to reunite Hills with the water-meadows below.

Hills was the ancient playground of the College, in the centuries before playing fields and all the other recreational facilities of the modern school. It was on top of Hills, for example, that the earliest forms of what has now become formalized as Winchester College Football were first played, probably in the seventeenth century. Ascending the south slope, from the point where the towpath ends, nowadays we can climb a substantial set of wooden steps leading right up to the Iron Age ditch and rampart. At the very centre is a clump of beeches, beneath whose roots lie the now invisible ruins of an eleventh century Norman chapel. To the north-east of Clump is a curious maze, cut into the grass and chalk – 'Mizmaze' according to the Council's helpful guiding signs, or 'Labyrinth' to generations of more classically-minded Wykehamists. It was probably first cut in the late seventeenth century, and is based on a loose design of nine 'nesting', or concentric, squares, which may conceivably have some connection with the ancient game of Nine Mens' Morris, or possibly with a similar design found on the floor of Chartres Cathedral.

Until the twentieth century, the school's right to use Hills as its playground was precarious, and even occasionally contentious. The ancient custom of organized expeditions to Hills was finally abolished with the advent of Dr Ridding's new playing fields. However, in order to assert the College's continuing legal rights over Hills, Ridding's successor Dr Fearon established the 'modern' custom, which still continues today, of the now annual migration of the entire school to the top of Hills – in recent years, on Ascension Day. The Headmaster no longer reads Psalm 121 ("I will lift up mine eyes unto the hills …"), but the Prefect of Hall still calls the school roll, and the young gentlemen descend to breakfast, prescriptive rights (in days gone by) duly asserted. Since 1930, when the Old Wykehamist Masonic Lodge bought the freehold of Hills from the Church and presented it to the College, the ceremony has ceased to have any legal relevance, but the tradition continues nonetheless.

The panorama of Winchester from Hills has changed substantially in some respects since Radclyffe's illustration 160 years ago. Great vistas of housing stretch out to the east, and even more to the west. The skyline of upper Winchester to the north-west is conspicuously broken by the County Hospital, the Prison's Hanging Tower and the Police Headquarters. But, to today's spectator just as much as to Radclyffe, it is the huge, benignly louring bulk of the Cathedral which still dominates the picture: Hills is a rare spot from which the magnificence of the Cathedral's exterior can be fully appreciated. And in another respect the view today is the same as it was in Radclyffe's time: the City of Winchester may lie before us, but in every direction we see greenery: the water-meadows directly below us, the playing fields beyond, a universal impression of trees, with a notable profusion almost completely masking the heart of the College, and rural Hampshire rolling into the northward distance.

One other group of buildings stands out, from our vantage point. Away to the left and due west of the top of Hills, about half a mile to the south of Garnier Road and now at the southern extremity of built-up Winchester, stand the Church and Hospital of St Cross, and it is there that we shall end this stroll. We retrace our steps to Garnier Road and Logie, and then turn south for the bare half mile to St Cross – the river and water-meadows to our left, intermittent houses and allotments to our right – following the same route as inspired Keats, on Sunday 19 September 1819, subsequently to write '*To Autumn*'.

New Field and St. Catherine's Hill

The original Hospital of St Cross was built between 1133 and 1136, the creation of Henry de Blois, grandson of the Conqueror and himself Bishop of Winchester from the precocious age of 28. It comprises a fine Transitional Norman church, which was begun in 1135 and only completed at the end of the next century (with subsequent alterations), and the Hospital, whose principal surviving buildings date from the fourteenth and fifteenth centuries. Throughout nearly 900 years of existence, for better or for worse, the Hospital has been a living institution, offering a haven for elderly gentlemen; it was, if you like, the prototype Sheltered Housing scheme. There are up to 25 Brothers: not more than 17 from the original Foundation of Henry de Blois, who wear a black gown with a silver cross, and not more than eight from the Order of Noble Poverty, which was founded 300 years later by Cardinal Beaufort, identifiable by their crimson gowns and cardinal's badges. Nowadays each Brother has his own one-bedroom flat, or quarter, although there are also communal facilities and duties. The Gaudy Lunch, held three times a year in the mid-fourteenth century Brethren's Hall, is a particularly conspicuous event in the communality of the Hospital. To become a Brother, a man has to be 60 or more, of good character and able-bodied; there are no other formal qualifications, and today's Brothers come from all walks of life and all parts of the country.

If all that sounds familiar, and stirs recollections of a different Hospital in another (fictional) Wessex cathedral city, it is well-established that Trollope based Hiram's Hospital in Barchester on St Cross. The original Charter of St Cross contemplated 'thirteen poor men' as resident Brethren, and the feeding of 'one hundred other [non-resident] poor persons', but the observance and implementation of the Charter over the following centuries was heavily dependent on the very variable probity of successive Masters. Sir Roger de Cloune (1370-74), a particularly notorious Master, evicted most of the Brethren, reduced the 100 non-resident diners to two or three begging scraps at the gate, and by selling off as much property as he could (for his own gain) had virtually destroyed the Hospital before he was ousted and the Hospital was restored to greater propriety and prosperity. The most notorious (and also most long-serving) Master, whose conduct inspired Trollope's 'The Warden', was Francis North, later Earl of Guilford: he held the post from 1807 to 1855, leaving the running of the Hospital to a chaplain and steward while extracting the maximum revenue from the Hospital's property for his own benefit. He too was eventually ousted, but only after a lengthy and expensive court action, also mentioned by Trollope. Happily, the Hospital has enjoyed much better fortune over the following 150 years, both spiritually and materially, and today's visitor will find the tranquillity for which Dr Harding so wistfully yearned in Barchester, in those earlier days of his own Wardenship, before Mr Bold's agitations.

We could not leave St Cross and end this stroll without experiencing the unique and ancient tradition for which the Hospital is widely famed – the Wayfarer's Dole. Any passing traveller, requesting refreshment, has always been given it, willingly and freely. Originally the refreshment might well have been a bottle of wine and a loaf of bread. Today, when the only call for the Dole is from less needy tourists like ourselves, we get just a token 'morsel of bread and horn of beer', but the tradition of hospitality continues unabated in this beautiful and timeless oasis of peace by a Hampshire water-meadow.

St. Cross

Note

Not all of the places described in this book are open to the public. In some cases, permission will need to be sought. It may not always be granted. Some of the places described, while open to the public, have only limited opening hours.

The Porters' Lodge is the starting point for guided tours round the College. Its telephone number is **01962 621227**. Further information about the College, including arrangements for access, can be found on the College's website, **www.winchestercollege.org**.

Information about access to the Cathedral can be obtained from the Cathedral Office. Its telephone number is **01962 857200**. The Cathedral's website is at **www.winchester-cathedral.org.uk**.

For information about the City generally, the telephone number of the City Tourist Information Centre is **01962 840500**, and its website is at **www.visitwinchester.co.uk**

Winchester
An illustrated stroll through City and College
First published September 2005
By Wykeham Publishing, Trout Cottage, Stockbridge, Hampshire, SO20 6EX
Text © Rupert Hill 2005
Illustrations © Dennis Page 2005

ISBN 0-9551039-0-8

Printed by BAS Printers, Salisbury, Wiltshire
Typeset in 11/13pt Garamond MT

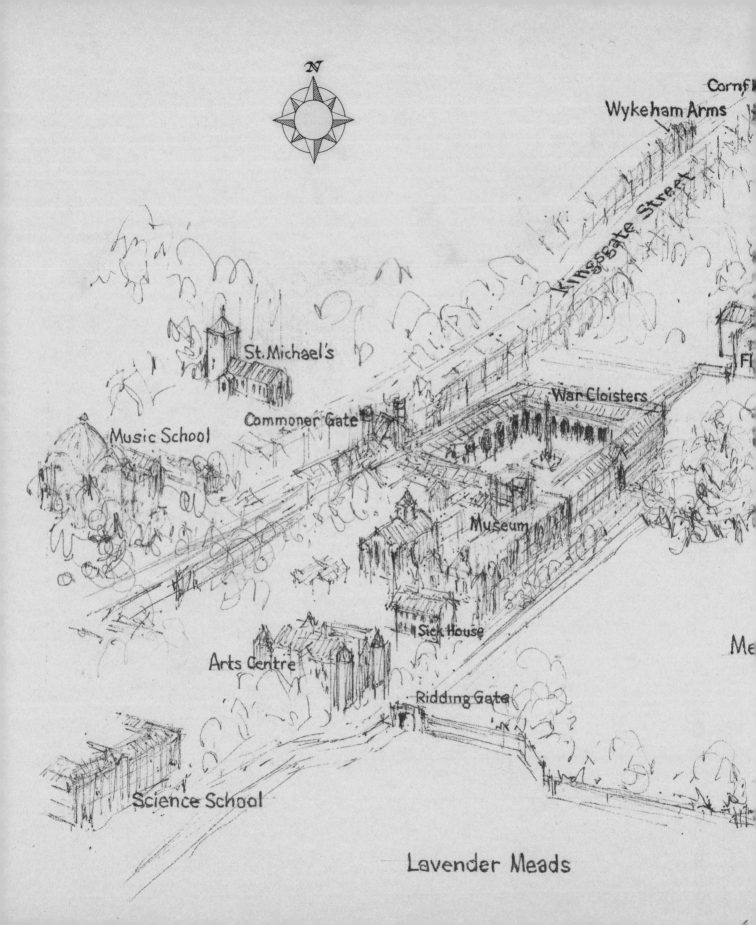

N

Cornf[...]

Wykeham Arms

Kingsgate Street

St. Michael's

War Cloisters

Music School

Commoner Gate

F[...]

Museum

Me[...]

Sick House

Arts Centre

Ridding Gate

Science School

Lavender Meads